When the Iron Bird Flies

And horses run on wheels, the Tibetan people will be scattered like ants across the face of the earth and the dHarma will come to the land of the red man

PADMASAMBHAVA 8TH CENTURY A.D.

I believe,
not a fanatical belief
and not blind faith
but in humanity
in what we can do for each other
in what we can do for the earth.
I believe in life
life after life
our only life.
To live for future generations,
we must decide now
if they are to inherit
freedom
or
chaos
BEN HARPER

When Danny Clinch approached us with the idea for this book we were excited. We knew that there would be no better way to depict the people, experience and spirit of the Tibetan Freedom Concerts than with this collection of his incredible photographs.

The photos in this book tell the story of not only the bands that have donated their talent to the cause, but also of the thousands of people on both sides of the stage who have become friends of Tibet through the concerts. From sound men and lighting technicians, to volunteers and concert goers, to musicians and artists, the people in Danny's pictures have all contributed to the great success of the Tibetan Freedom Concerts, The Milarepa Fund, and the Tibetan Freedom movement as a whole.

The Milarepa Fund was founded in 1994 with a mission to try and help the Tibetan people regain their freedom by raising awareness and encouraging people to take action for Tibet. Inspired by the Tibetan people's commitment to nonviolence and compassion, The Milarepa Fund's campaigns have tried to honor the example that the Tibetans have set during the brutal Chinese occupation of their country.

The time, energy, and goodwill contributed to the Tibetan Freedom Concerts by Danny and all those involved have been recognized by Tibetans and Tibet supporters around the world, and most importantly, by those Tibetans still inside Tibet. Everyone who has attended, worked on or supported the Tibetan Freedom Concerts has contributed to the Tibet work that keeps the spirit of hope alive, a hope that ensures Tibet will soon be free.

This book is dedicated to all Tibetans both inside and outside of Tibet and to all those who support their right to freedom.

SIX PRINCIPLES OF NONVIOLENCE

1 Nonviolence is not passive, but requires courage

2 Nonviolence seeks reconciliation, not defeat of an adversary

3 Nonviolent action is directed at eliminating evil, not destroying an evil-doer

4 A willingness to accept suffering for the cause, if necessary, but never to inflict it

5 A rejection of hatred, animosity or violence of the spirit, as well as refusal to commit physical violence; and

6 Faith that justice will prevail.

The fundamental tennets of Dr. Martin Luther King Jr.'s philosophy of nonviolence described in his first book, *Stride Toward Freedom*.

CHAKSAM-PA 1997 NEW YORK CITY

TIBET ON THE LINE

March 10, 1959
Thousands of Tibetans rise up in a massive protest to the occupation of their country. Over 80,000 are killed and many more are imprisoned. The Dalai Lama and most of the government officials are forced to flee to India.

1965
The Chinese government renames Tibet the "Tibetan Autonomous Region."

March 8, 1989
Increased Chinese government repression leads to massive demonstrations. Martial law is declared. Pictures from these events and the three days of riots that ensue are published in the West, giving the outside world a picture of what the Chinese government has done to Tibet.

1966 - 1969
China's Cultural Revolution spreads to Tibet. Tibetans are forced to publicly renounce their religion, culture, and government. Many Tibetans are imprisoned, tortured, and killed for not conforming.

1949
The Chinese government moves large numbers of troops into Tibet.

1959 - 1965
The United Nations passes three resolutions condemning the Chinese government's atrocities in Tibet.

June 4, 1989

Thousands of Chinese democracy student protesters are killed in Tiananmen Square by the People's Liberation Army of China. The grim reality of the Chinese government's heavy hand is seen by the world media and international community.

October 1989

The Dalai Lama is awarded the Nobel Peace Prize for his tireless work in seeking a peaceful resolution to the Tibetan situation through dialogue.

March 10, 1998

On the anniversary of the 1959 Uprising, six Tibetan refugees begin a hunger strike unto death in New Delhi. Their demand is that the issue of Tibet be revisited by the United Nations General Assembly. After 49 days without food, the strikers are forcibly hospitalized by the Indian police. In response, 50 year old Tibetan activist, Thupten Ngodup, sets himself on fire and dies from his burns.

June 24, 1998

In an unprecedented live broadcast of a press conference between the Presidents of China and the United States, the issue of Tibet is brought up, marking the first time ever that the Tibet issue has been publicly debated in China.

1999

The 50th anniversary of the invasion comes at a time when public outcry for Tibet is louder than ever. The Tibetans have not, and will not, give up hope that Tibet will be free.

1996 SAN FRANCISCO

There's this really cool note in the dressing room saying, *PLEASE LEAVE YOUR EGO AT THE DOOR,*
and everybody seems to be doing just that. It's absolutely wild. There's a really, really positive feeling
...and it really feels good.
THOM YORKE

10

1999 CHICAGO

This is a very tangible event, an opportunity to feel the power of activism. *ERIN POTTS*
Co-founder of The Milarepa Fund

1996 SAN FRANCISCO

What we need to work for is Human Rights for everyone.
We mustn't allow one person or one race to have his or her Human Rights taken away.
When ONE person's freedom is lost, it deprives us ALL of freedom.

PALDEN GYATSO

If Tibetans are able to gain their freedom,
it is going to be an example to the rest of the world that nonviolence is a viable way of bringing about change.
The media is so important because the Tibetans' only weapon is truth.

ADAM YAUCH

From participating in the past two freedom concerts,
I have learned what's going on in Tibet now, and what went on there in the past.
If Tibet is destroyed, we will lose one of the most important achievements in human history:
the values of nonviolence and compassion that have been cultivated over centuries in Tibet.

SEAN LENNON

1997 NEW YORK CITY

I am speaking for all Tibetans still in prison and for all Tibetans that have ever been in prison...
behind my voice lays the suffering of the thousands of prisoners who have not survived...
Our collective will to resist what is unjust is like a fire that cannot be put out.

PALDEN GYATSO

TIBET'S REALITY

Tibetan musician and Fulbright Scholar, Ngawang Choephel and the
11th Panchen Lama of Tibet, as recognized by His Holiness the Dalai Lama are two of hundreds
political prisoners being held in Tibet today.
Usually these prisoners have taken part in demonstrations against the
Chinese government and have been convicted of fictitious charges

Possessing a photo of the Dalai Lama is currently illegal
and could result in imprisonment and torture.

$\mathcal{M}$ay 9 1996

I am hopeful that you will learn more about Tibet from your
participation in the June 15-16, 1996, Tibetan Freedom Concert in
the San Francisco Bay Area. On this occasion I extend my greetings
to you all. I also wish success for this event, organized by The Milarepa
Fund, a San Francisco-based non-profit organization dedicated to
the promotion of universal compassion through music.

I have always believed that any effort at highlighting the issue of
Tibet should be nonviolent. A concert is a very creative means to
achieve that. I am confident that this concert will inspire people,
especially the youth, to actively engage in supporting our struggle
for freedom and preservation of the ancient and rich Tibetan culture,
which has the potential to serve humanity at large.

Both personally, and on behalf of the six million suffering Tibetans, I
take this opportunity to express our gratitude to all the bands and
participants at the Tibetan Freedom Concert for sharing their talent
and time for this humanitarian initiative. We are also deeply
encouraged by the efforts of The Milarepa Fund in making the
Tibet concert a reality.

With my prayers and good wishes,

Yours sincerely,

The Dalai Lama

Without a free and democratic China,
Tibet cannot be free.
Without a free Tibet, China cannot be truly free.
And, unless we help other people's freedom,
we ourselves cannot be truly free... so *FREE TIBET*!

XIAO QIANG

Executive Director of Human Rights in China

DEMONSTRATIONS
Gatherings and protest activities organized to build support for peace, justice or social reform.

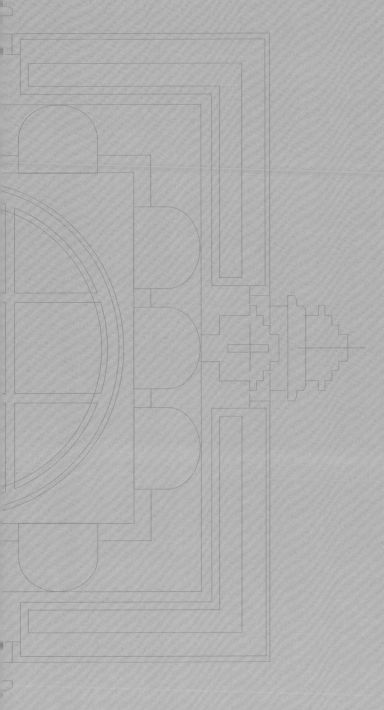

CIBO MATTO 1996 SAN FRANCISCO

We sing this song of sadNess
We sing it from Drapchi prison
Joy and happiness
aRe as high as sNow capped Mountains
We sing this song of indepeNdence

This song was sung by young Tibetan nuns in prison. As a result, nine years were added to their prison terms.

THE FUGEES 1996 SAN FRANCISCO

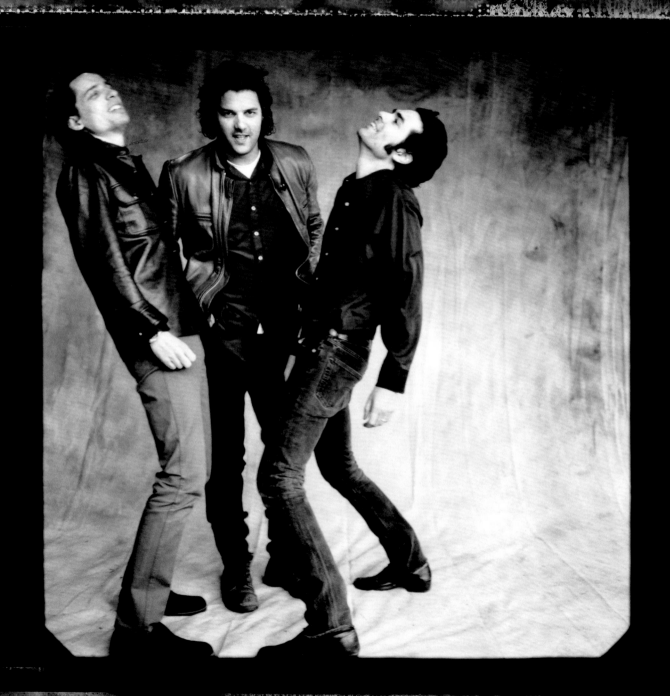

PORNO FOR PYROS 1997 NEW YORK CITY

CIVIL DISOBEDIENCE
Deliberate breaking of an unjust law,
including submitting to imprisonment if necessary,
to protest an injustice.

CHAKSAM-PA 1997 NEW YORK CITY

In December of 1948, the

Universal Declaration of Human Rights
was signed by nations around the world.
It was and is a document created from the ideal that all people are born equal and deserving of these fundamental rights.
Still, *fifty years later,* the declaration has a long way to go.
In many ways it is a document born out of the privileged western world.
They are the rights of *all* individuals but
the Reality of so few.

We look at our own situations as Afro-Americans and we are not going through near what the Tibetans are going through.
The way that they go about and choose to handle their problem could perhaps inspire everybody else in the world.
We are going to try and take this message home and maybe it can help us in our own situations and communities.
You have to realize that standing up for what you feel is right does not mean you have to put your fists up.

POSDNUOS & MASEO

The *UDHR* Guarantees Everyone

1 The *RIGHT* to equality
2 FREEDOM from discrimination
3 The *RIGHT* to life, liberty, and personal security
4 FREEDOM from slavery
5 FREEDOM from torture or degrading treatment
6 The *RIGHT* to recognition as a person before the law
7 The *RIGHT* to equality before the law
8 The *RIGHT* to remedy by a competent tribunal
9 FREEDOM from arbitrary arrest or exile
10 The *RIGHT* to a fair and public hearing
11 The *RIGHT* to be considered innocent until proven guilty
12 FREEDOM from interference with privacy, family, home or correspondence
13 The *RIGHT* to free movement in and out of any country
14 The *RIGHT* to asylum in other countries from persecution

15 The *RIGHT* to a nationality and freedom to change it
16 The *RIGHT* to marriage and family
17 The *RIGHT* to own property
18 FREEDOM of belief and religion
19 FREEDOM of opinion and information
20 The *RIGHT* of peaceful assembly and association
21 The *RIGHT* to participate in Government and free elections
22 The *RIGHT* to social security
23 The *RIGHT* to desirable work and to join trade unions
24 The *RIGHT* to rest and leisure
25 The *RIGHT* to an adequate standard of living
26 The *RIGHT* to education
27 The *RIGHT* to participate in the cultural life of a community
28 The *RIGHT* to social order assuring Human Rights
29 The opportunity to take part in community duties which are essential to free and full development
30 FREEDOM from state or personal interference in the above rights

To be ONE, to be united is a great thing,
but to respect the right to BE different is maybe even greater.

BONO

1997 NEW YORK CITY

1999 CHICAGO

FREE
TIBET

Many Politicians claim they do not need to spend much time working for Human Rights. We are here to remind them
that working for Human Rights is to work for all of us;
they are working on behalf of humanity.

WEI JINGSHENG
Chinese Democracy Activist and Former Political Prisoner

1998 WASHINGTON DC

1998 WASHINGTON DC

Everyone can make a difference for Tibet.
Where you spend your money makes a difference, who you vote for makes a difference.
JOHN ACKERLY
President of the International Campaign for Tibet

1998 WASHINGTON DC

There are lots of crap reasons to be a rock star. This is one of the good ones.   *THOM YORKE*

1997 NEW YORK CITY
1996 SAN FRANCISCO

I think Tibet can be freed without violence.
It'll take large numbers of people using whatever means they're able to,
either boycotts or writing letters to elected officials or electing people who are willing to ACT responsibly.

ADAM YAUCH

88

There is a mentality where people THINK that by just going to the concert, that has sorted that problem out.
All the prisoners are out of jail NOW and all the hungry are fed.
And of course it isn't that way.
But it's a great START.   *BONO*

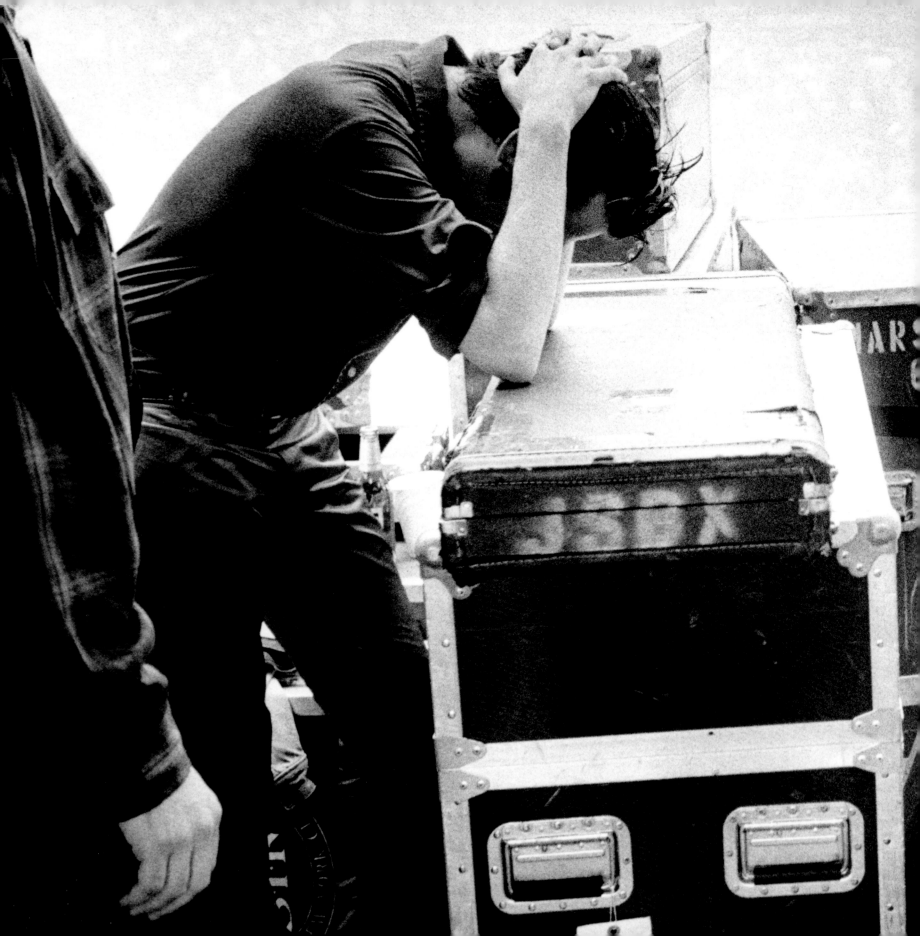

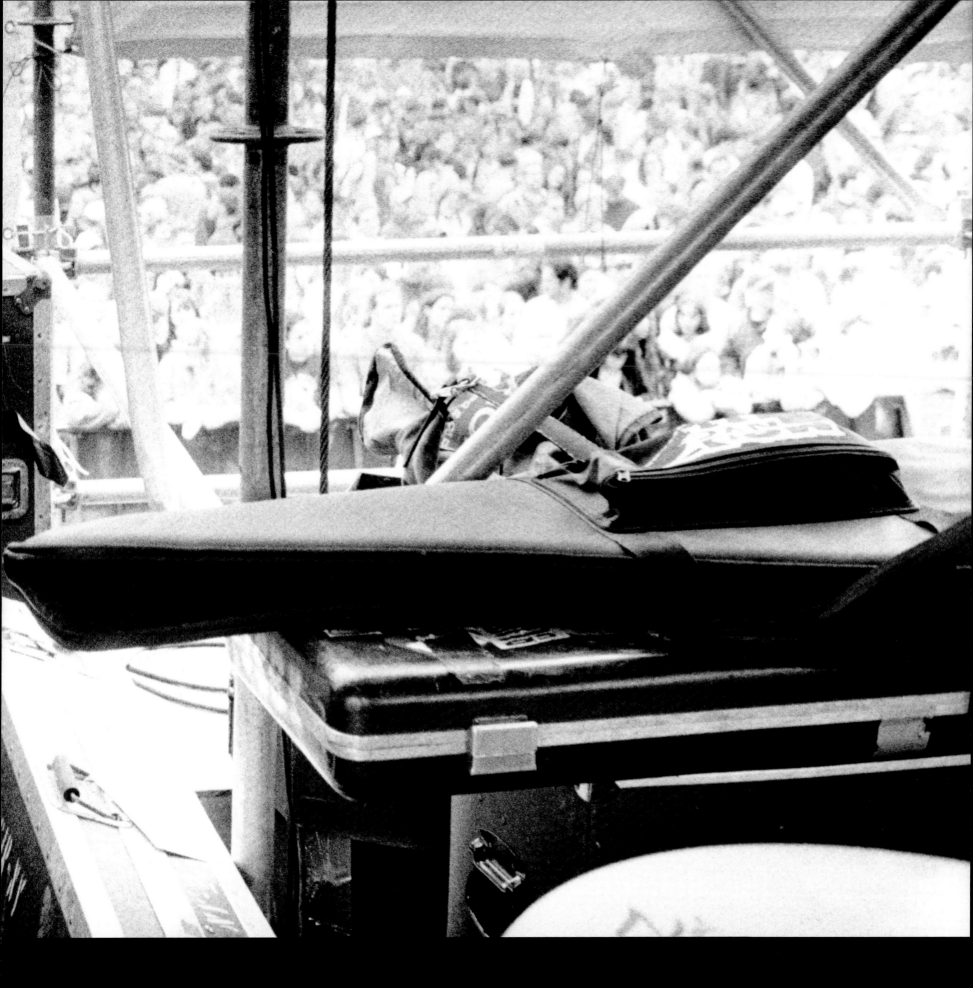

TIBET'S REALITY

Forced abortions and sterilizations are common in Tibet,
as teams of mobile clinics move through the countryside to some of the most remote communitie
Pregnant women are subject to abortions,
without warning or consent, regardless of the term of pregnancy.

Population transfer into Tibet is quickly making Tibetans a minority in their own country
China offers economic incentives to Chinese settlers who agree to move to this remote land.
Tibetans are outnumbered 2 to 1 in Lhasa, the capital city.

$\mathcal{A}$pril 8 1997

In my own limited experience, the basic source of all happiness is love and compassion, a sense of kindness and warm-heartedness towards others. If you can be friendly and trusting towards others, you become more calm and relaxed. You lose the sense of fear and suspicion that we often feel about other people, either because we don't know them well or because we feel they are threatening or competing with us in some way. When you are calm and relaxed you can make proper use of your mind's ability to think clearly, so whatever you do you will be able to do it better. Nonviolence is something more meaningful than the mere absence of violence. It means that if you can help and serve others you should do so. If you cannot, you should at least restrain yourself from harming them. Moreover, nonviolence is not restricted merely to other human beings. It also has to do with ecology, the environment and our relations with all the other living being with whom we share the planet. Positive attitudes like kindness, friendliness and concern for others are not a luxury but a condition for health and happiness.

I am greatly encouraged that there is to be a second Tibetan Freedom Concert. It gives me great pleasure to know the cause of Tibet has such strong support from young people. At this concert, I am sure you will also at the same time enjoy yourselves. I am reminded that in old Tibet there was nothing people liked better than to have a picnic, to get together and enjoy themselves. I feel these concerts are taking place in the same spirit. What the Tibetan people urgently need is hope and encouragement. They will find this if they feel they have friends and I have no doubt that the Tibetan Freedom Concert is a loud expression of friendship.

Yours sincerely,

The Dalai Lama

I am here in the United states,
where *I* have freedom of speech
and the right to practice my religion.

I am asking for help on behalf of all Tibetans
for these same basic human rights.

DADON | 1997 NEW YORK CITY

Reggae has always been the voice of the oppressed. If one of us is not free, then no one is free.

MUTABARUKA

DIRECT ACTION
Organized, nonviolent resistance to injustice. More than 250 forms of nonviolent direct action have been identified.

CHUCK D 1997 NEW YORK CITY

SONIC YOUTH 1997 NEW YORK CITY

WARREN HAYNES 1998 WASHINGTON DC

More than ever before, our world needs Tibet.
In an age marked by increasing acts of brutality and violence,
we need the principles on which this peaceful and compassionate culture are based.
More than ever before, the Tibetan people need you.
They need your energies. They need your talents. They need your hope and your freedom to insure they are not forgotten.

LHADON TETHONG
Students for a Free Tibet

FOO FIGHTERS 1996 SAN FRANCISCO

NEGOTIATIONS
Process of discussing, compromising and bargaining with
adversaries in good faith to secure a resolution to a conflict.

MONKS, NUNS, & ADAM YAUCH 1997 NEW YORK CITY

As a student I was constantly reading about horrible things that had happened in the past.
People regretted it.   Here it is happening right now. You don't need to regret it; you can just do something.
Now is the time and Tibet is a perfect way to right so many wrongs that have gone on in the past.

DECHEN WANGDU

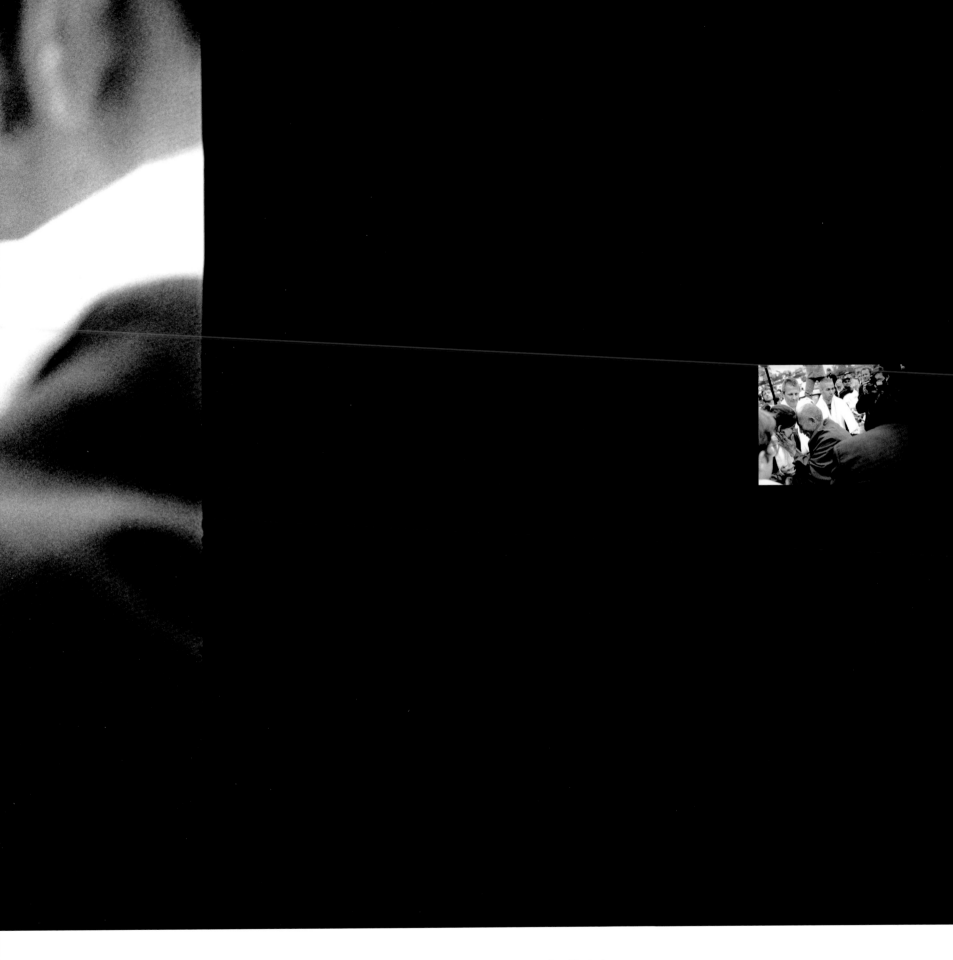

To see all the faces of the youth gathered here today will probably be the greatest moment of my life. And to see you all here for freedom and peace brings my heart to the greatest heights.

PALDEN GYATSO

1996 SAN FRANCISCO

Tibet is always looked at as this Shangri-La. Tibet is definitely a spiritual land, but we are in an urgent situation.
Please don't think of it only as a romantic place, but also as a place where people must struggle to survive.

TASHI DHONDUP OF CHAKSAM-PA

*I think that people should get their R*ump *S*haking *on, but with the mind set of thinking about compassion, awareness, and nonviolence.*

MIKE D

1996 SAN FRANCISCO

TIBET'S REALITY

Tibetan children are forced to attend Chinese schools and learn to read and write in Chinese. Many Tibetan young are unable to speak their own language.

As a result, thousands of Tibetan children are sent over the Himalayas in hopes of gaining a Tibetan education in the Tibetan refugee schools in India and Nepal.

Tibetan monks and nuns are not able to freely practice their religion.

They are often forced to publicly denounce the Dalai Lama and their activities are closely monitored.

Most displays of Buddhist practices are primarily allowed for the sake of tourism.

The Tibetan Freedom Concerts earlier held in 1996 at
San Francisco and in 1997 at New York were extremely successful
and attracted a lot of media attention thus promoting wider
awareness about the non-violent Tibetan struggle for freedom.
These are a source of great encouragement for us and especially
for the Tibetan people living inside Chinese-occupied Tibet.
I would therefore like to appeal to the youth of today to actively
support the just cause of Tibet. I am confident that your actions will
compel your leadership to put more pressure on the totalitarian
Chinese government to respect human rights and freedoms
of the Tibetan people.
I am fully convinced that it is because of our non-violent struggle
that a growing number of Chinese, including those inside China,
are also showing their sympathy and concern for Tibet. I consider
this extremely important and significant. Through our non-violent
struggle for freedon we are also setting an example and thus
contributing to the promotion of a global political culture of
non-violence and dialogue.
I would like to express personally, and on behalf of the six million
suffering Tibetans, our sincere appreciation and gratitude to all the
participants and especially the artists performing at the Tibetan
Freedom Concert. I hope your event will motivate more people
to engage in active support for Tibet.

With my prayers and good wishes,
Yours sincerely,

The Dalai Lama

I THINK MUSIC BY IT'S VERY NATURE IS POLITICAL.

MICHAEL STIPE
1997 NEW YORK CITY

TIBET'S REALITY
Tibetans are discriminated against and face various forms of racism in their own country.
Employment opportunities are given to the Chinese settlers as incentives to remain in Tibet.
Most businesses are Chinese owned and operated.
All signs must be printed in Chinese. Many Tibetans are reduced to begging in the street.

Over 100,000 Tibetans have followed the Dalai Lama into exile.
They continue to demonstrate against the Chinese occupation of Tibet and attempt to gain support
from people and governments around the world. Tibetans and their supporters
encourage the Chinese government to begin a dialogue with the Dalai Lama.

$\mathcal{M}$arch 10 ^{19}99

Excerpts from His Holiness the Dalai Lama's March 10th
statement marking the 40th anniversary of Tibet Uprising Day.
On March 10th, 1959, hundreds of thousands of Tibetans
demonstrated against the Communist Chinese Government's
occupation of Tibet. Thousands of Tibetans were killed
and thousands more imprisoned.

...The plight of the Tibetan people and our non-violent freedom
struggle has touched the hearts and conscience of all people who
cherish truth and justice. The international awareness of the issue of
Tibet has reached an unprecedented height since last year.
Concerns and active support for Tibet are not confined to human
rights organizations, governments and parliaments. Universities,
schools, religious and social groups, artistic and
business communities as well as people from many other walks of
life have also come to understand the problem of Tibet and are
now expressing their solidarity with our cause...
Today, the Tibetan freedom movement is in a much stronger and
better position than ever before and I firmly believe that despite
the present intransigence of the Chinese government, the
prospects for progress in bringing about a meaningful dialogue and
negotiations are better today than ever. I, therefore, appeal to
governments, parliaments and our friends to continue their
support and efforts with renewed dedication and vigor.
With my homage to the brave men and women of Tibet, who have
died for the cause of our freedom, I pray for an early end to the
suffering of our people.

His Holiness The Dalai Lama

I feel that music is the last true voice of the human spirit.

It is the last voice that can go beyond language, beyond age, and beyond color straight to the heart and mind of all people and therefore, its power is immeasurable.

BEN HARPER

1997 NEW YORK CITY

I think that the DAY will come very soon
when we'll be able to put on the
TIBET IS FREE CONCERT

ERIN POTTS
Co-founder of The Milarepa Fund

CONCERTS

San Francisco

Polo Fields, Golden Gate Park
June 15th & 16th 1996
$800000 raised
Over 100000 Attendees

Speakers: Chimi Thonden-Tibetan Activist, Palden Gyatso-Former Political Prisoner, Shen Tong-Chinese Democracy Activist, Robert A.F. Thurman-Professor of Indo-Tibetan Buddhist Studies, Columbia University

The Smashing Pumpkins, Foo Fighters, Chaksam-pa, Beastie Boys, A Tribe Called Quest, Pavement, Cibo Matto, Biz Markie, Richie Havens, John Lee Hooker, Red Hot Chili Peppers, Rage Against the Machine, Sonic Youth, Beck, Björk, De La Soul, The Fugees, Buddy Guy, The Skatalites, Yoko Ono/Ima

New York City

Randall's Island
June 7th & 8th 1997
$250000 raised
Over 50000 Attendees

Speakers: Palden Gyatso-Former Political Prisoner, Dechen Wangdu-Tibetan Activist, Chuck D-Public Enemy, Xiao Qiang-Human Rights in China, Nane Alejandrez-Barrios Unidos

Foo Fighters, U2, Sonic Youth, Biz Markie, Alanis Morissette, Patti Smith, The Jon Spencer Blues Explosion, Radiohead, Yungchen Lhamo, Ben Harper & The Innocent Criminals, A Tribe Called Quest, Beastie Boys, Rancid, Björk, Pavement, Blur, Michael Stipe & Mike Mills, Taj Mahal & The Phantom Blues Band, De La Soul, Dadon, Chaksam-pa, Nawang Khechog, The Mighty Mighty Bosstones, Eddie Vedder & Mike McCready, KRS-One, Rancid, Noel Gallagher, Sonic Youth, Porno for Pyros, Lee Perry featuring Mad Professor and the Robotiks Band

Washington DC

RFK Stadium
June 13th & 14th 1998
$1.2 Million raised
Over 120000 Attendees

Speakers: Xiao Qiang-Human Rights in China, Lhadon Tethong-Students for a Free Tibet, Palden Gyatso-Former Political Prisoner, Wei Jingsheng-Chinese Democracy Activist and Former Political Prisoner

Radiohead, Sean Lennon, Mutabaruka, Money Mark, A Tribe Called Quest, Dave Matthews Band, Sonic Youth, Nawang Khechog, Wyclef Jean, Herbie Hancock and the Headhunters, Buffalo Daughter, R.E.M., KRS-One, Beastie Boys, The Wallflowers, Blues Traveler, Live, Pearl Jam, Luscious Jackson, Red Hot Chili Peppers, Chaksam-pa, Pulp

4 cities
June 12th 1999
$150000 raised
Over 55000 Attendees

Chicago

Alpine Valley Music Theatre

Speakers: Xiao Qiang-Human Rights in China, Lhadon Tethong-Students for a Free Tibet, Nawang Pema-Tibetan Nun

Run DMC, The Cult, Beastie Boys, Blondie, Tracy Chapman, The Roots, Live, Eddie Vedder, Otis Rush, Cibo Matto, Handsome Boy Modeling School, Rage Against the Machine, Chaksam-pa

Amsterdam

Rai Parkhal

Speakers: Erin Potts-The Milarepa Fund, Ama Adhe-Former Political Prisoner.

Garbage, Blur, Urban dance Squad, Alanis Morissette, Ben Harper & The Innocent Criminals, Luscious Jackson, NRA, Gangchenpa, Tibetan Institute of Performing Arts, Joe Strummer & The Mescaleros, Thom Yorke

Tokyo

Tokyo Bay NK Hall

Speakers: Alma David-Students for a Free Tibet, Gurme Wangda-Liason Office of His Holiness the Dalai Lama

Hi-Standard, Buffalo Daughter, Brahman, Audio Active, Kan Takagi, Scha Dara Parr, Kiyoshirou Imawano, Nawang Khechog

Speakers: Lobsang Lungtok-Former Political Prisoner, Jo Shaw-Students for a Free Tibet, Australia, Dorji Dolma-Australia Tibet Council

Sydney

Sydney Show Grounds

Regurgitator, Spiderbait, The Mavis's, The Avalanches, Neil Finn, The Living End, Celibate Rifles, Not From There, Gerling, Jebediah, You Am I, Garpa, Blackalicious, Eskimo Joe, Trans Am

It's georgeous out here today.
 People are listening to music and becoming aware of a way of life to do with peace, compassion and tolerance.
Man, when you get those things combined with 120,000 young people, you're on your way.
PERRY FARRELL

Cover Beck
San Francisco 1996

5 Chaksam-pa
New York City 1997

6 Demonstrators
San Francisco 1996

7 Demonstrators
San Francisco 1996
Cops
New York City 1997

8 Thurston Moore, Sonic Youth
San Francisco, 1996

10 John Merithew, Eddie Vedder, Brad Balsley
Chicago 1999

11 Eddie Vedder and Security
Chicago 1999

12 Mike Diamond, Beastie Boys
Adam Yauch, Beastie Boys
Washington DC 1998

13 Mike Diamond
Adam Yauch
Washington DC 1998

14-15 Audience
Chicago 1999

16 Joe Sirois, Dicky Barrett,
The Mighty Mighty Bosstones
Adam Yauch
New York City 1997

17 Marky Ramone, The Ramones
Howie Pyro
Lars Frederikson, Tim Armstrong, Rancid
New York City 1997

18 Adam Yauch
San Francisco 1996

20 Nuns
Chicago 1999

21 Stupa
San Francisco 1996
Volunteer
New York City 1999
Ed Kowalczyk, Live
Ian Astbury, The Cult
Chicago 1999

22-23 Press Conference
New York City 1997

24-25 Monks and Nuns
New York City 1997

26-27 Sean Lennon
The Jon Spencer Blues Explosion
Nuns
New York City 1997
Blues Traveler
Rick Rubin
Washington DC 1998
Mike Mills and Michael Stipe
New York City 1997

28-29 Monastery Tent
Chicago 1999

30 Karma Gyaltsen, Chaksam-pa
San Francisco 1996

31 Palden Gyatso
San Francisco 1996

33 Monks
San Francisco 1996

34 Ian Astbury, The Cult
Chicago 1999

35 Phurbu Tsering, Chaksam-pa
New York City 1997

36 Yoko Ono
San Francisco 1996

37 Sean Lennon
San Francisco 1996

38 Richie Havens
San Francisco 1996

39 KRS-One
New York City 1997

40 D'arcy, The Smashing Pumpkins
San Francisco 1996

41 James Iha, The Smashing Pumpkins
San Francisco 1996

42 Anthony Keidis, Red Hot Chili Peppers
Washington DC 1998

43 Colin Greenwood and Jonny Greenwood,
Radiohead
Washington DC 1998

45 Nawang Khechog
New York City 1997

46 Chaksam-pa
New York City 1997

47 Toby Morse, H2O. Tattoo by Civ
New York City 1997

48 Beastie Boys
New York City 1997

49 Cibo Matto
San Francisco 1996

50 Tim Armstrong
New York City 1997

51 Pat Smear, Foo Fighters
San Francisco 1996

We have been supportive of people throwing off the yoke of oppression wherever it is.

TOM MORELLO

Rage Against the Machine

52 De La Soul
San Francisco 1996

53 Security
New York City 1997

54 Michael Stipe and Thom Yorke
New York City 1997

55 Luscious Jackson
Washington DC 1998

56 Mike McCready and Eddie Vedder
New York City 1997

57 Money Mark
Washington DC 1998

58 Spike Jonze
San Francisco 1996

59 Ed McGinty, Spike Jonze,
Sienna McLean, Michelle DiLorimer
San Francisco 1996

61 Monks and Nuns
Chicago 1999

62 Chaksam-pa
San Francisco 1996

63 The Fugees
San Francisco 1996

64 The Jon Spencer Blues Explosion
New York City 1997

65 Porno for Pyros
New York City 1997

66 Rage Against the Machine
Chicago 1999

67 Rage Against the Machine
Chicago 1999

69 Chaksam-pa
New York City 1997

70-71 John Hancock
San Francisco 1996 / Chicago 1999
Security
Washington DC 1998
Event Staff
San Francisco 1996
Buffalo Daughter
Washington DC 1998
Event Staff
Audience
San Francisco 1996
Chad Taylor, Live, and Ruby
Washington DC 1998

73 Bono, U2
New York City 1997

75 Event Staff
Chicago 1999

76-77 Thom Yorke, Radiohead
1998 Washington DC 1998

78 Monks and Nuns
Chicago 1999
Yungchen Lhamo
Chuck D
New York City 1997

79 Capitol Building
Washington DC 1998
Ben Harper
New York City 1997

80 Eun Young Lee
Washington DC 1998
Nun
New York City 1997

81 Demonstration
Washington DC 1998

82 Timo Ellis, Cibo Matto
Washington DC 1998

83 Pulp
Washington DC 1998

84 Alfredo Ortiz, Beastie Boys
Chicago 1999

85 Matt Sweeney
Washington DC 1998

86 Adam Yauch
San Francisco 1996

87 Cops
San Francisco 1996

88 Erin Potts, Chuck D, Adam Yauch
New York City 1997
Demonstrators
San Francisco 1996

89 Cops
New York City 1997

90 Bono
Fans
New York City 1997

91 Sean Lennon
New York City 1997

92-93 Jon Spencer
New York City 1997

94-95 Ian Astbury
Chicago 1999

96 Alanis Morissette
New York City 1997

97 Dadon
New York City 1997

99 Mutabaruka
Washington DC 1998

100 Kesang Lamdark
Washington DC 1998

101 Ed Kowalczyk, Live
Washington DC 1998

102 Todd Oldham
New York City 1997

103 Anna Sui
San Francisco 1996

104 Chris Shaw
Washington DC 1998

105 Sonam Topgyal
Washington DC 1998

106 Rolando Alphonso O.D., The Skatalites
San Francisco 1996

107 Buddy Guy
San Francisco 1996

109 Sam Chapin
Chicago 1999

110-111 Eddie Vedder
Chicago 1999

112 Chuck D
New York City 1997

113 Adam Yauch
San Francisco 1996

114 Sonic Youth
New York City 1997

115 Nuns
New York City 1997

116 Björk
San Francisco 1996

117 Radiohead
Washington DC 1998

118 Robert A.F. Thurman
San Francisco 1996

119 Photo Tent
Washington DC 1998

120 The Mighty Mighty Bosstones
New York City 1997

121 Kevin Lenear, The Mighty Mighty Bosstones
New York City 1997

122 ?uestlove, The Roots
Chicago 1999

123 Run DMC
Chicago 1999

124 Blues Traveler
Washington DC 1998

125 Warren Haynes
Washington DC 1998

126 Damon Albarn, Blur
New York City 1997

128 Pavement
San Francisco 1996

129 Foo Fighters
San Francisco 1996

131 Thom Yorke
Washington DC 1998

133 Monks, Nuns,
Adam Yauch
New York City 1997

134-135 Jon Spencer and Cristina Martinez
A Tribe Called Quest
New York City 1997
?uestlove
Chicago 1999
Dadon
New York City 1997
Live
Chicago 1999

136-137 Billy Corgan
San Francisco 1996

138-139 Palden Gyatso
San Francisco 1996

140 Audience
Chicago 1999

141 Eddie Vedder
Chicago 1999

142 Milarepa Staff
San Francisco 1996

143 Milarepa Staff & Production crew
Washington DC 1998

144 Beck
John Lee Hooker
San Francisco 1996

145 John Lee Hooker
San Francisco 1996

146 Monk
New York City 1997

147 Sonam Tashi
San Francisco 1996

148-149 Beastie Boys
Chicago 1999

150 Beastie Boys
Chicago 1999

We want to change the world. We can change the world because we are young.

XIAO QIANG
Executive Director of Human Rights in China

186

151　Beastie Boys
　　　Chicago 1999

152-153　Beastie Boys
　　　Chicago 1999

154　Tim Armstrong
　　　New York City 1997

155　Audience
　　　San Francisco 1996

156　Taj Mahal
　　　New York City 1997

157　Taj Mahal
　　　Björk
　　　Kevin Lenear
　　　New York City 1997

158-159　Otis Rush
　　　Chicago 1999

160-161　Palden Gyatso, Adam Yauch, Monks
　　　New York City 1997

162　Nuns
　　　New York City 1997

163　Michael Stipe
　　　New York City 1997

164　Q-Tip, A Tribe Called Quest
　　　New York City 1997

165　Ali, A Tribe Called Quest
　　　New York City 1997

166　Money Mark
　　　Washington DC 1998

167　Yangsi Rinpoche
　　　Chicago 1999

168　Medic
　　　San Francisco 1996

169　Biz Markie
　　　New York City 1997

170　Björk
　　　New York City 1997

171　Beck
　　　San Francisco 1996

172　Cop
　　　New York City 1997

173　Rick Rubin
　　　Washington DC 1998

174　Namgyal Lhamo and Chukie Tethong,
　　　Chaksam-pa
　　　New York City 1997

175　Ben Harper
　　　New York City 1997

176-177　Nuns
　　　Washington DC 1998

180-181　Krist Novoselic, Danny Clinch, Ed Smith
　　　Washington DC 1998
　　　Sonic Youth
　　　New York City 1997
　　　Chacksam-pa
　　　Washington DC 1998

182-183　Perry Farrell
　　　Washington DC 1998
　　　Milarepa Staff & Production crew
　　　Chicago 1999
　　　Audience
　　　San Francisco 1996
　　　Gary Ashley
　　　Chicago 1999

184-185　Shelby Meade
　　　Steve Martin, Shelby Meade, Perry Serpa
　　　Chicago 1999
　　　Danny Clinch
　　　New York City 1997
　　　Deyden Tethong and Lhadon Tethong
　　　Washington DC 1998
　　　Crazy Legs and Maria Ma
　　　Chicago 1999
　　　Evan Bernard
　　　New York City 1997
　　　Money Mark
　　　Chicago 1999

186-187　Maurice Menares
　　　New York City 1997
　　　J.C. Callendar, Deyden Tethong,
　　　Stacy Horne, Josh Schrei
　　　Chicago 1999
　　　Alanis Morissette
　　　Tim Armstrong
　　　New York City 1997
　　　Christopher Thorn and Heather Thorn
　　　Washington DC 1998
　　　Nasty Little Man staff
　　　Chicago 1999
　　　Perry Farrell
　　　Washington DC 1998
　　　Ed Smith
　　　San Francisco 1996

188-189　Amy Finnerty
　　　Washington DC 1998
　　　Danny Clinch and Maria Barba
　　　New York City 1997
　　　Dechen Wangdu and Tenzin Losel
　　　Chicago 1999
　　　Walker Banard
　　　San Francisco 1996
　　　Kurt Langer
　　　Erica Maeyama and Josh Schrei
　　　Stacy Horne
　　　Washington DC 1998
　　　Dustin Rabin, Peter Ross, Gary Ashley
　　　Chicago 1999

191　RFK Stadium
　　　Washington DC 1998

Back cover　Palden Gyatso
　　　San Francisco 1996

The Monks and Nuns who performed at the Tibetan Freedom Concerts have represented Sere Je Monastery,
The Tibetan Nuns Project, Drepung Loseling Monastery, and Kopan Nunnery as well as several other institutions. We thank them all
for their generous involvement over the years.

Thanks to God and my Family. Love to Maria, Max, and Marina.
Special thanks to those people in my studio, Lisa Connelly, Hannah Connors, and Lindha Narvaez, who worked their tails off
to put this project together.
Danny would also like to thank The Milarepa Fund, Steve Martin, Shelby Meade, Perry Serpa and Nasty Little Man,
Chris Covert, Jill Ellefson, Elizabeth Grubaugh, Dustin Rabin, Gary Ashley, Peter Ross, Ed Smith. Extra large thank you's from Danny to
Jeff Dachis, Craig Kanarick, Michael Simon, Lisa Shimamura, RSUB, and all those who's efforts contributed to the making of this book.

RSUB
107 Grand Street New York, NY 10013

RSUB is a subnetwork of talent, ideas, and relationships that
creates and distributes entertainment in all forms, including books,
music, clothing, film, and digital media. For more information
about RSUB, visit www.rsub.com.

The Milarepa Fund is dedicated to helping the Tibetan people
regain their freedom through education and nonviolent activism.
For more information about The Milarepa Fund, visit
www.milarepa.org

Photographs by Danny Clinch
Edited by Danny Clinch & Elizabeth Grubaugh

Production Managers: Lisa Shimamura, Deyden Tethong,
Andrew Bryson
Creative Direction & Design: Elizabeth Grubaugh
Production Design: Paul Pollard, Tomo Makiura
Editing: Deyden Tethong, Andrew Bryson, Lisa Shimamura
Design Assistance: Yuu Anai, Chiemi Sugimoto
Production Assistance: Chris Smyk, Noah Dachis, Evan Fisher,
Matthew Stinchcomb, Gabriel Rivera, Brian Poillon
Photographs Printed by Jeffrey Kane, Edge Custom Lab (B & W),
Anthony Accardi, Green Rhino (Color), Kevin Amer (Polaroid)
Color Processing by Riaz Hamed & C-Lab
Printed by CS Graphics, Singapore
Paper is 170gsm Leykam mat

ISBN 0-9664100-4-1

Tibetan Freedom Concerts 1996-1999
When the Iron Bird Flies © 2000
Danny Clinch Photography, Inc.

Published by Razorfish Studios, Inc. in New York City

Library of Congress Card Number: 00-102874

First Edition September 2000

I was drawn to this project through music and a chance to photograph those musicians I admire.
I was offered an all-access photo pass as long as I could get myself to San Francisco
to shoot the first Tibetan Freedom Concert. I asked if I could set-up a portrait tent and I was
certain the answer would be "no." They said "yes." I was also asked to photograph the press conference.
For me this was the turning point, listening to the statements made at the press conference.
How could anyone not be moved by the lack of Human Rights in the lives of these people,
rights that anyone I've ever known has had.
Although my knowledge of the issues increases daily, I will not pretend to know every intricate detail
of this struggle, but I will offer these photographs as a document of the efforts of so many dedicated individuals
to raise awareness, as a step towards the fulfillment of Human Rights for everyone.

DANNY CLINCH

The proceeds from the Tibetan Freedom Concerts have enabled The Milarepa Fund to continue its work in support of the Tibetan people's nonviolent struggle for freedom. The Milarepa Fund has donated much of this money directly to organizations working for nonviolence around the world and to the Tibetan communities in exile.

The Northern Land of the world is Tibet…

The summit of snow which touched the sky
                                    Is matchless insight without equal.

                        The sun and moon turning around its peak
Are meditation radiating wisdom and compassion.

                The Light filling space
                            Is Compassion dispelling the darkness of ignorance.

                                JETSUN MILAREPA
                            11th Century Tibetan Saint